FIVE-DOLLAR BILLS

BY MADDIE SPALDING

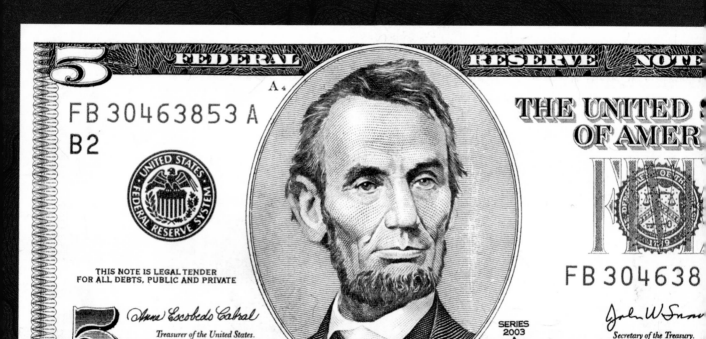

The Child's World®
childsworld.com

Published by The Child's World®
1980 Lookout Drive • Mankato, MN 56003-1705
800-599-READ • www.childsworld.com

Photographs ©: Brian McEntire/Shutterstock Images, cover
(foreground), cover (background), 1 (foreground), 1 (background);
Bernhard Richter/Shutterstock Images, 5; Steve Stock/Alamy, 6, 7,
20 (middle), 20 (bottom); Norman Chan/Shutterstock Images, 9;
iStockphoto, 10, 15; Andrei Tudoran/Shutterstock Images, 12–13;
Shutterstock Images, 16–17, 20 (top); Everett Historical/Shutterstock
Images, 19; Red Line Editorial, 22

Design Elements: Brian McEntire/Shutterstock Images; Ben Hodosi/
Shutterstock Images

ISBN 9781503820098
LCCN 2016960496

Printed in the United States of America
PA02336

ABOUT THE AUTHOR

Maddie Spalding writes and
edits children's books. She lives
in Minnesota.

TABLE OF CONTENTS

CHAPTER ONE

WHAT IS A FIVE-DOLLAR BILL?. 4

CHAPTER TWO

SECURITY FEATURES. 8

CHAPTER THREE

THE HISTORY OF THE FIVE-DOLLAR BILL 14

TIMELINE 20

FAST FACTS 21

WHERE MONEY IS MADE. . .22

GLOSSARY 23

TO LEARN MORE 24

INDEX 24

WHAT IS A FIVE-DOLLAR BILL?

Five-dollar bills are a type of money. Five one-dollar bills equal one five-dollar bill. The Bureau of Engraving and Printing (BEP) makes five-dollar bills. Bills are made from cotton and **linen**.

The BEP makes more than two billion five-dollar bills each year.

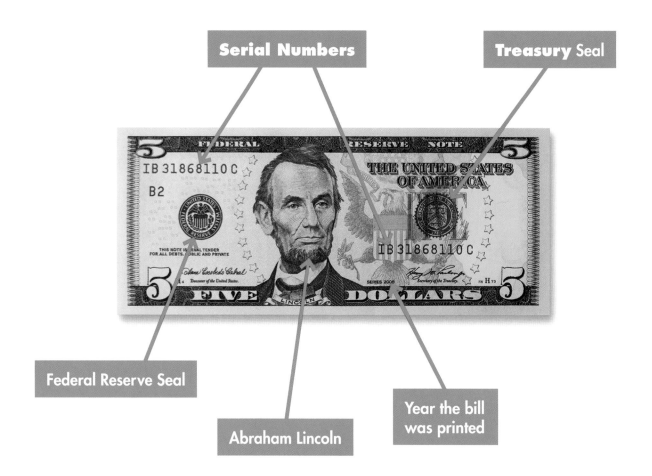

Serial Numbers

Treasury Seal

Federal Reserve Seal

Abraham Lincoln

Year the bill was printed

Former president Abraham Lincoln is on the front of the five-dollar bill.

Why do you think the Lincoln Memorial
is on the back of the five-dollar bill?

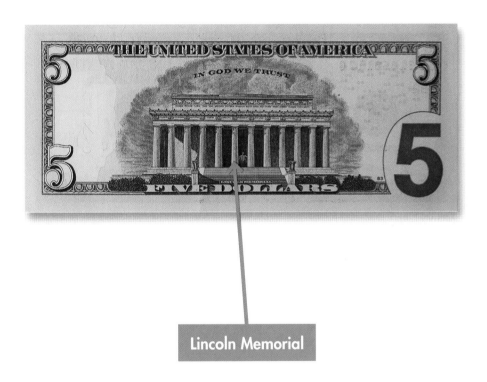

Lincoln Memorial

The Lincoln **Memorial** is on
the back.

CHAPTER TWO

SECURITY FEATURES

Five-dollar bills have serial numbers. Each bill has a different serial number.

The first letter of serial numbers identify which Federal Reserve Bank gave out the bill.

The security thread appears on the left side of the five-dollar bill.

Each five-dollar bill has a security thread. This thread glows blue under a certain type of light.

These features make it more difficult for people to make fake five-dollar bills.

Not all U.S. bills have the same security features. Why do you think this is true?

Another security feature is the U.S. Department of the Treasury seal.

CHAPTER THREE

THE HISTORY OF THE FIVE-DOLLAR BILL

The first U.S. five-dollar bills were made in 1861. Alexander Hamilton was on the front. He was one of the Founding Fathers of the United States.

Many people have been featured on the five-dollar bill. Former president Andrew Jackson was on the front of the five-dollar bill in 1907.

The **design** on the five-dollar bill changed many times. Chief Running Antelope was put on the front of the bill in 1899. He was a Sioux chief. He was known for his bravery.

Chief Running Antelope was the leader of the Hunkpapa Sioux Tribe.

Abraham Lincoln first appeared on the five-dollar bill in 1914. The Lincoln Memorial was put on the back of the bill in 1929.

Why do you think Abraham Lincoln appears on the five-dollar bill?

ABRAHAM LINCOLN was

the 16th president of the United States
(1861–1865). He held the country together
during the U.S. Civil War.

1861 The first U.S. five-dollar bills were made. Alexander Hamilton was on the front.

1899 U.S.
five-dollar bill

1899 Sioux Chief Running Antelope was put on the front of the five-dollar bill.

2006 U.S.
five-dollar bill

1914 Abraham Lincoln first appeared on the five-dollar bill.

Back of a 2006
five-dollar bill

1929 The Lincoln Memorial was put on the back of the five-dollar bill.

★ The U.S. Treasury plans to reveal new designs for the back of the five-dollar bill in 2020. The designs will show events that happened at the Lincoln Memorial, such as Martin Luther King Jr.'s "I Have a Dream" speech.

★ Eight people have appeared on the U.S. five-dollar bill: Abraham Lincoln, Alexander Hamilton, Andrew Jackson, Ben Harrison, Sioux Chief Running Antelope, George Thomas, James Garfield, and Ulysses Grant.

★ Chief Running Antelope was the first Native American to appear on U.S. money.

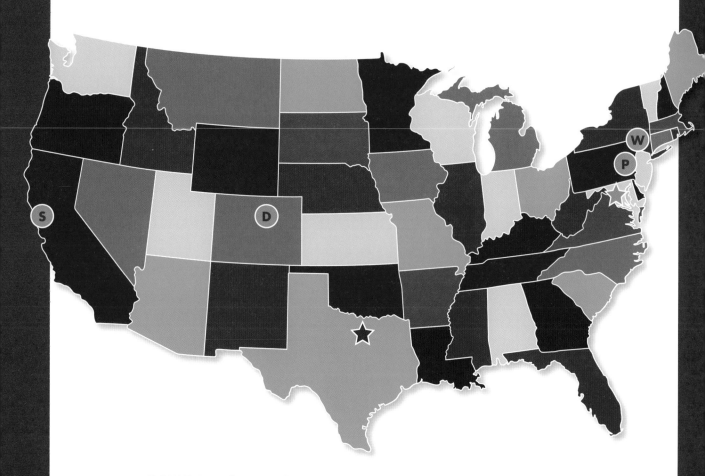

BUREAU OF ENGRAVING AND PRINTING OFFICES

⭐ Fort Worth, Texas

⭐ Washington, DC

COIN-PRODUCING MINTS

Ⓓ Denver, Colorado—Produces coins marked with a D.

Ⓟ Philadelphia, Pennsylvania—Produces coins marked with a P.

Ⓢ San Francisco, California—Produces coins marked with an S.

Ⓦ West Point, New York—Produces coins marked with a W.

design (di-ZINE) A design is the shape or style of something. The U.S. five-dollar bill design has changed many times.

linen (LIN-uhn) Linen is a strong type of cloth. Five-dollar bills are made from cotton and linen.

memorial (muh-MOR-ee-uhl) A memorial is built to honor something. The Lincoln Memorial is on the back of the five-dollar bill.

serial numbers (SEER-ee-ull NUM-burz) Serial numbers are numbers that identify something. Five-dollar bills have serial numbers.

Treasury (TREZH-ur-ee) A Treasury is a part of a government that is in charge of a country's money. The U.S. Department of the Treasury is in charge of money in the United States.

IN THE LIBRARY

Gilpin, Caroline Crosson. *Abraham Lincoln*.
Washington, DC: National Geographic, 2012.

Jozefowicz, Chris. *10 Fascinating Facts about Dollar Bills*.
New York, NY: Children's Press, 2017.

Schuh, Mari C. *Counting Money*.
Minneapolis, MN: Bellwether, 2016.

ON THE WEB

Visit our Web site for links about five-dollar bills:
childsworld.com/links

Note to Parents, Teachers, and Librarians: We routinely verify our Web links to make sure
they are safe and active sites. So encourage your readers to check them out!

INDEX

Bureau of Engraving and
   Printing, 4
Chief Running Antelope, 16
cotton, 4
design, 16
Federal Reserve Seal, 6
Hamilton, Alexander, 14

history, 14–19
Lincoln, Abraham, 6, 18–19
Lincoln Memorial, 7, 18
linen, 4
security thread, 11
serial numbers, 6, 8
Treasury Seal, 6